What's in My Classroom?

by Kim Young

NATIONAL GEOGRAPHIC LEARNING | CENGAGE Learning

Hi. This is my classroom.
Let's play a game.

2

It's on the wall.
It's a circle.
What is it?

It's a clock.

It's small.
It's yellow.
What is it?

It's a pencil.

It's big.
It's a rectangle.
What is it?

It's the board.

It's small.
It's green.
What is it?

It's Shelly!
She's our turtle.

Facts About Clocks

There are different ways to show time on a clock.

This is one o'clock.

This is two o'clock.

What time is this?

There are many different kinds of clocks.

cuckoo clock

alarm clock

wall clock

wrist watch

What kinds of clocks do you have in your home?

Fun with
Classroom Objects

What is it? Match the words to the pictures.

pencil

board

clock

turtle

Look at the pictures.
Find the words.

pencil

b	q	c	p	c
o	c	l	e	i
a	x	o	n	r
r	l	c	c	c
d	d	k	i	l
a	l	l	e	

board

circle

clock

Glossary

big

game

play

small

wall